To: Darling Mano

With lots of love
from: Chuty Amma,
Uncle Mevan
& Avanthi.

08/25/2005

Chinese
Brain
Twisters

Chinese Brain Twisters

(Originally published as *Chinese Brain Twisters*
and *More Chinese Brain Twisters*)

Over 100 Puzzles
Fun for the Whole Family!

Baifang

BARNES
&NOBLE
B O O K S
NEW YORK

Contents

Contents

Introduction

There is wisdom in the old Chinese saying "Things learned during childhood remain with one forever." When I was growing up in the north of China during the 1950s and 1960s, my family and friends taught me many of the puzzles included in this book. My parents recalled others from their childhood in the 1930s and 1940s.

Such puzzles are part of China's folk culture. They have endured for centuries, even through the Communist era of Mao Zedong, when so many other traditional ways of life were lost. They speak of the commitment of most Chinese parents to expand their children's intellectual capacities during even their earliest years.

Hoping to bring this tradition to my adopted country, I collected some of the best puzzles to put in this small book. I hope you and your children enjoy them as much as I have.

Baifang

Instructions

The book is divided into three parts: Sticks and Shapes, Sticks and Numbers, and Words and Numbers. Each contains puzzles that help develop agile, creative minds. These mental calisthenics will also help prepare your child for a lifetime of clear, logical thinking. Playing with real sticks allows your child to manipulate the concepts and leads to even greater learning.

Who can solve these puzzles?

Anyone above the age of eight can enjoy the puzzles. When I was a child, my family introduced me to the easiest ones first. As I learned how to solve them, I tried to remember the solutions so that I could solve them faster the next time I saw them.

Although your child may work his or her way through the book alone, it is much more fun to share the experience. You can do these puzzles together at any place, at almost any time—at home, on vacation, on a plane or train, or even while camping. One person can work on them alone, of course, or a group can turn them into a game by competing against each other or against the clock.

What do you need to solve the puzzles?

You'll need a pen or pencil, some paper, and a flat surface. You'll also need about 50 short sticks. Toothpicks or matchsticks are just the right length. You can also use straws cut into equal lengths, about two inches long.

To solve the puzzles, form the patterns with your sticks or draw them on a piece of paper.

Rules for the puzzles:

To **move** sticks means to shift the position of a stick without reducing the original number.

To **remove** a given number of sticks means to take away, thus reducing the number of sticks in the pattern.

To **add** means to increase a given number of sticks.

Let's try one stick puzzle together:

These **three** diamonds can be changed into **four** equilateral (equal-sided) triangles by moving **two** sticks. Which **two** should be moved?

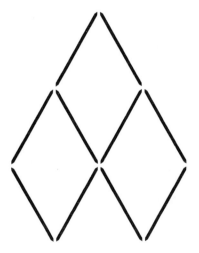

Turn the page to find the solution.

Start

Here the thick lines show the sticks to be moved.

Finish

And here the thick lines show the new position of the moved sticks.

Now let's begin!

Sticks and Shapes

By moving only **two** sticks, these **three** equal-sized squares can be changed into **four** equal-sized rectangles. Which **two** sticks should be moved?

Start

Finish

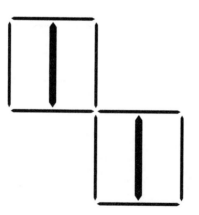

This Y-like figure can be turned upside down by moving **two** sticks. Which **two** should be moved?

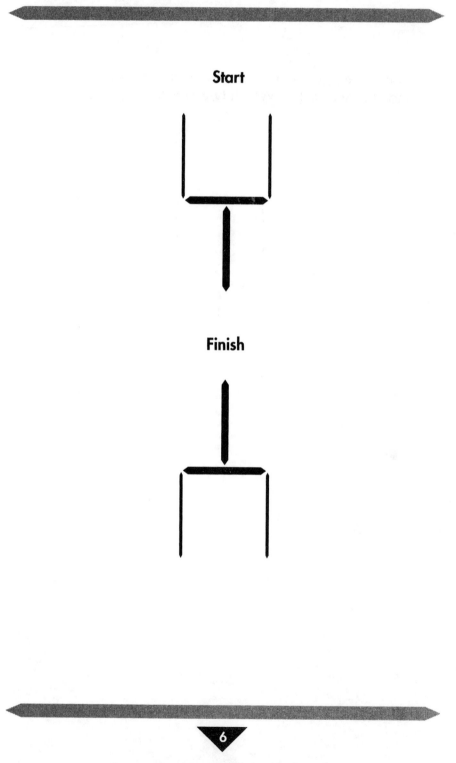

Start

Finish

This shovel is made of four sticks. How can these four sticks be made into a chair? How can they be made into a stool?

Start

Finish

Finish

CHAIR

STOOL

This pattern can be changed into **one** diamond and **one** equilateral (equal-sided) triangle by moving **two** sticks. Which **two** should be moved?

Start

Finish

By moving only **two** sticks, the gap at the bottom left corner of this pattern can be closed up, leaving **two** squares. Which **two** sticks should be moved?

Start

Finish

This house can be changed into **two** houses by moving only **one** stick. Which **one** should be moved?

Start

Finish

This pattern is made of **three** equal-sized rectangles. How can it be changed into **six** squares by moving only **three** sticks?

Start

Finish

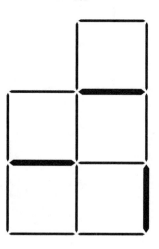

These two rectangles can be changed into **two** squares by moving **two** sticks. Which **two** should be moved?

Start

Finish

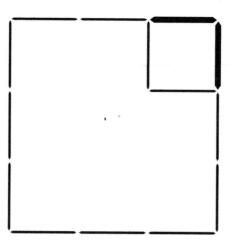

How can this pattern be changed into **three** squares by moving only **three** sticks?

(There is more than one solution.)

SOLUTION A

Start

Finish

SOLUTION B

Start

Finish

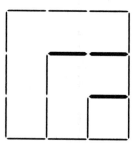

How can this dog be made to turn around by moving only **one** stick?

Start

Finish

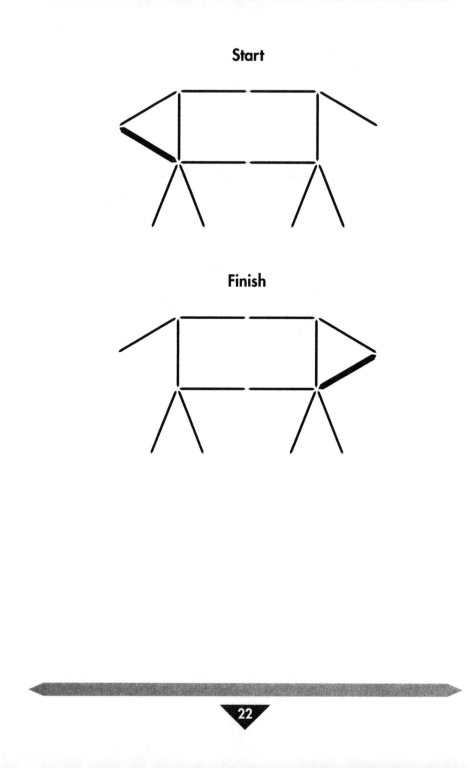

How can this dog be made to look back by moving only **two** sticks?

Start

Finish

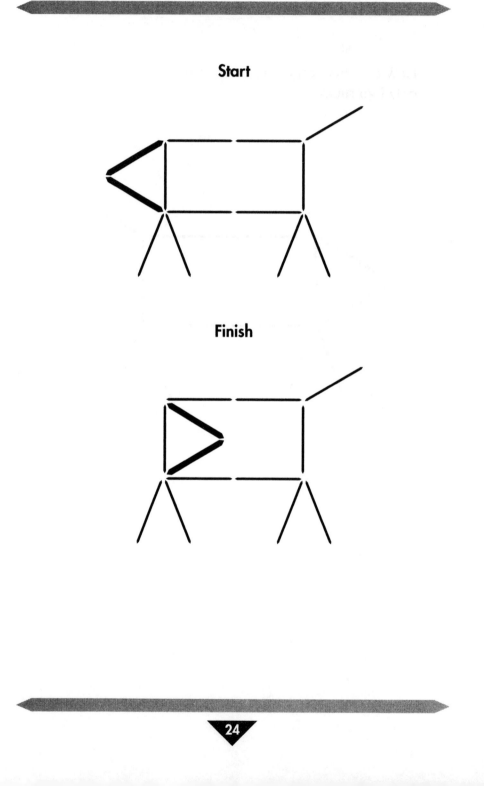

This pattern can be changed into a cube (three-dimensional square) by moving **three** sticks. Which **three** should be moved?

Start

Finish

This L-shaped pattern can be changed into **four** equal-sized squares by moving **four** sticks. Which **four** sticks should be moved?

Start

Finish

This L-shaped pattern can be changed into **four** equal-sized squares by moving only **two** sticks. Which **two** should be moved?

Start

Finish

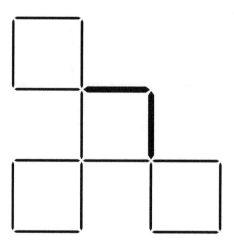

This L-shaped pattern can be changed into **three** squares by moving **four** sticks. Which **four** should be moved?

Start

Finish

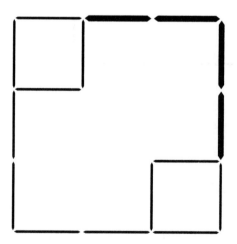

This L-shaped pattern can be changed into **two** squares by moving **six** sticks. Which **six** should be moved?

(There is more than one solution.)

SOLUTION A

Start

SOLUTION B

Start

Finish

Finish

This pattern can be turned **upside down** by moving **four** sticks. Which **four** should be moved?

Start

Finish

This equilateral (equal-sided) triangle can be changed into **five** equilateral triangles by moving **five** sticks. Which **five** should be moved?

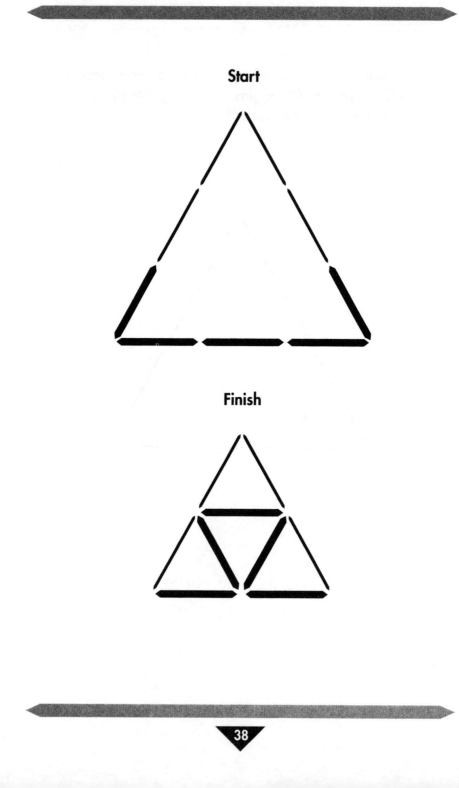

Start

Finish

This pattern can be changed into **six** equilateral (equal-sided) triangles by removing **three** sticks. Which **three** should be removed?

Start

Finish

This pattern can be changed into **five** equilateral (equal-sided) trianges by removing **four** sticks. Which **four** should be removed?

Start

Finish

1. This pattern is made of **six** equal-sized equilateral (equal-sided) triangles. By moving **two** sticks, it can be changed into **five** equal-sized equilateral triangles. Which **two** should be moved?

2. The resulting pattern of **five** equilateral triangles can be changed into **four** equilateral triangles by moving **two** sticks. Which **two** should be moved?

3. The resulting pattern of **four** equilateral triangles can be changed into **three** equilateral triangles by moving **two** sticks. Which **two** should be moved?

4. Finally, the pattern of **three** equilateral triangles can be changed into **two** equilateral triangles by moving **two** sticks. Which **two** should be moved?

Start   Finish

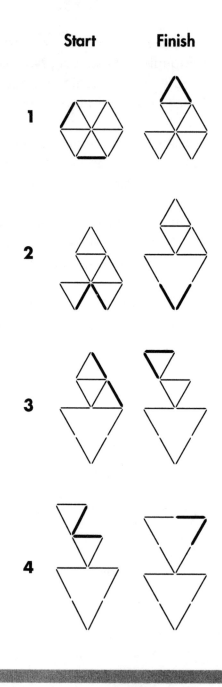

1

2

3

4

This pattern is made of **five** squares. By moving **eight** sticks, it can be changed into **nine** squares. Which **eight** should be moved?

Start

Finish

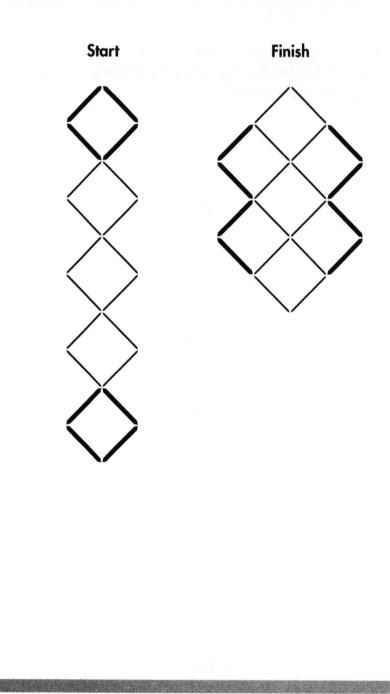

By moving **three** sticks, you can make this goldfish turn around and swim in the **opposite direction**. Which **three** should be moved?

Start

Finish

How can this pattern be changed into **five** equal-sized squares by removing **four** sticks?

Start

Finish

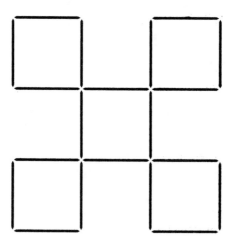

How can this pattern be changed into **three** squares by removing **six** sticks?

(There is more than one solution.)

SOLUTION A

Start

Finish

SOLUTION B

Start

Finish

SOLUTION C

Start

Finish

SOLUTION D

Start

Finish

How can this pattern be changed into **two** squares by removing **eight** sticks?

(There is more than one solution.)

SOLUTION A

Start

Finish

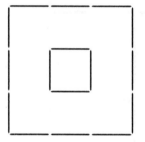

SOLUTION B

Start

Finish

The number of triangles in this pattern can be reduced to **four** by removing **four** sticks. Which **four** should be removed?

Start

Finish

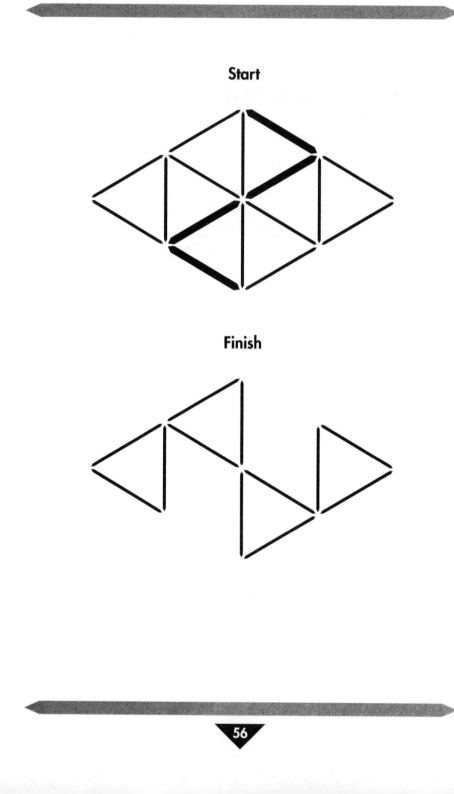

This table lamp can be changed into **five** triangles by moving **three** sticks. Which **three** should be moved?

Start

Finish

How can this pattern be changed into **six** diamonds by moving **four** sticks?

Start

Finish

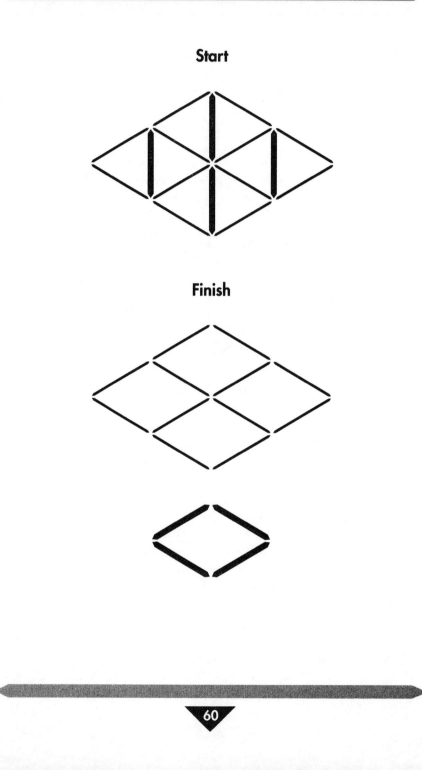

This key can be changed into **three** equal-sized squares by moving **four** sticks. Which **four** should be moved?

Start

Finish

This pattern can be changed into **nine** squares by moving **four** sticks. Which **four** should be moved?

Start

Finish

How can this pattern be divided into **four** identical shapes by adding **five** sticks?

Start

Finish

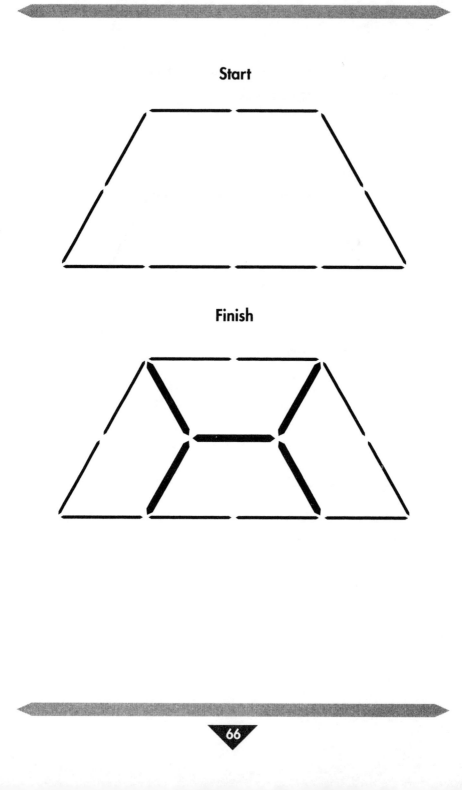

This pattern can be divided into **four** quarters by adding **eight** sticks. Where should the **eight** sticks go?

Start

Finish

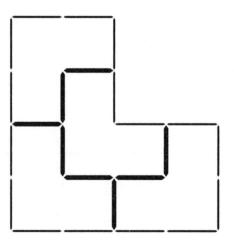

This pattern can be changed into **six** diamonds by moving **six** sticks. Which **six** should be moved?

Start

Finish

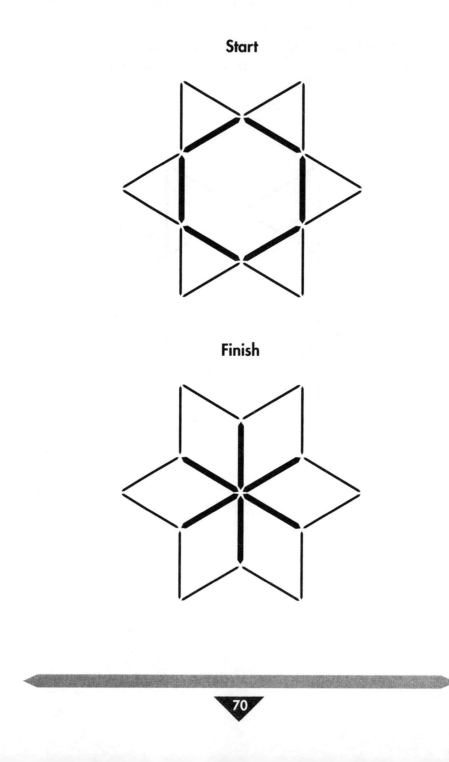

This equilateral (equal-sided) triangle can be divided into **three** identical shapes by adding **three** sticks. Where should the **three** sticks go?

Start

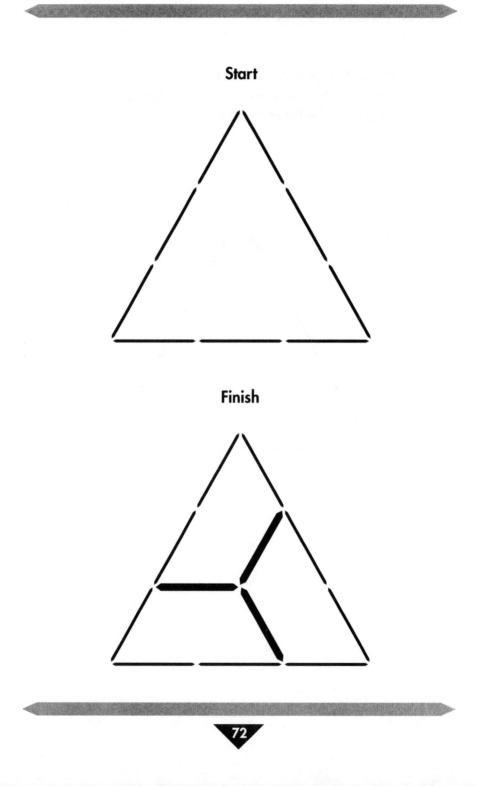

Finish

This pattern can be changed into **two** equal-sized triangles by moving **four** sticks. Which **four** should be moved?

Start

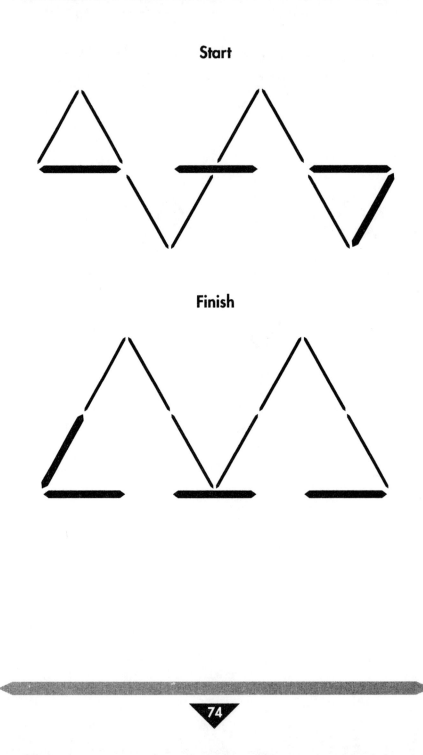

Finish

This Christmas tree can be changed into a goldfish by moving **two** sticks. Which **two** should be moved?

Start

Finish

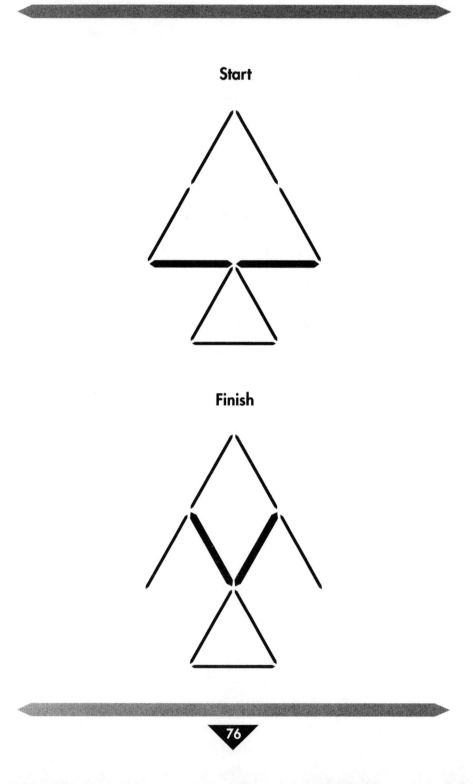

By moving **four** sticks, these **five** equal-sized squares can be reduced to **three** squares. Which **four** sticks should be moved?

Start

Finish

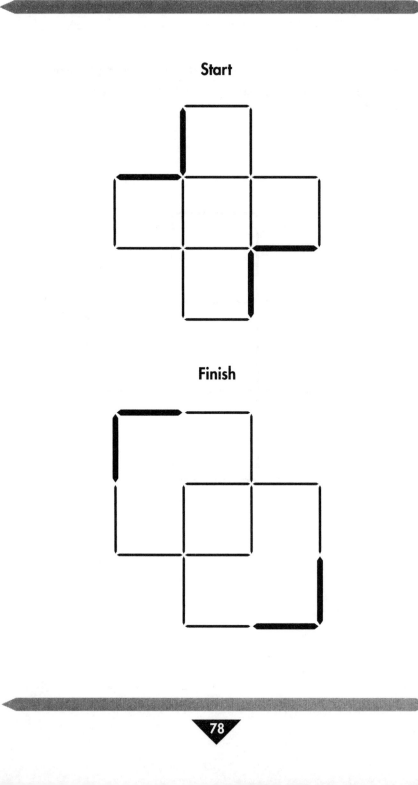

By adding **eight** sticks, this pattern can be divided into **three** identical shapes. Where should the **eight** sticks go?

Start

Finish

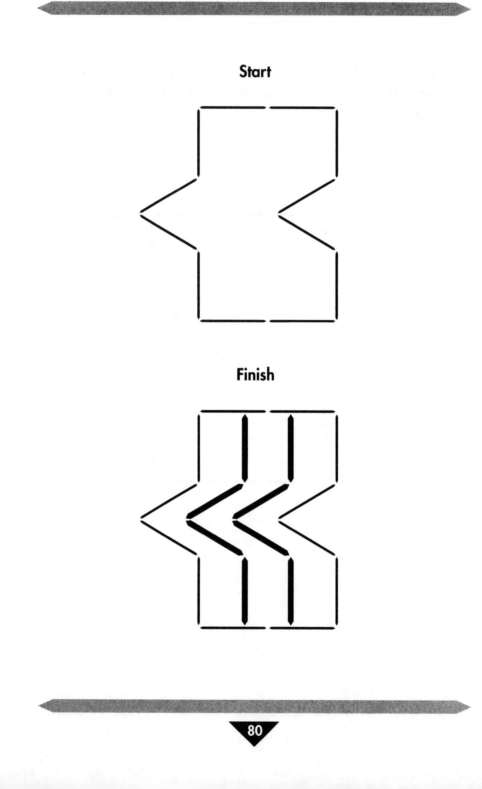

This pattern is made up of many squares. By removing **nine** sticks, it can be transformed into a pattern that will have **no squares** but **all rectangles**. Which **nine** should be removed?

Start

Finish

This pattern is made up of many squares. By removing **eight** sticks, it can be changed into **two** squares and **eight** equal-sized rectangles. Which **eight** should be removed?

Start

Finish

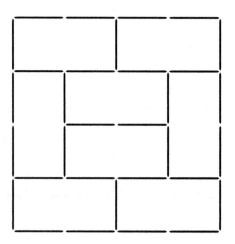

By removing **six** sticks, **half** of the equal-sized squares can be eliminated. Which **six** should be removed?

Start

Finish

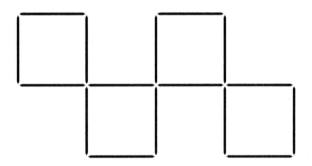

2

Sticks and Numbers

This math problem is incorrect, but moving only **one** stick will make it correct. Which **one** should be moved?

Start

Finish

This math problem is incorrect, but moving **one** stick will make it correct. Which **one** should be moved?

Start

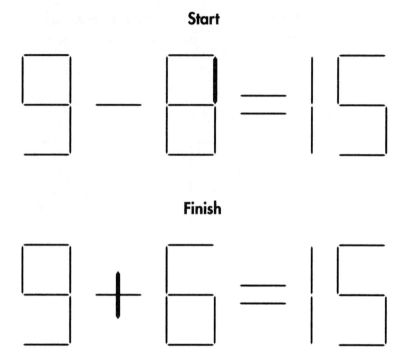

Finish

This math problem is incorrect, but moving **one** stick will make it correct. Which **one** should be moved?

99-59=10

Start

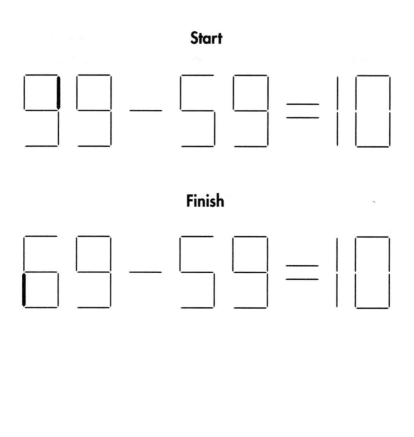

99 − 59 = 10

Finish

69 − 59 = 10

This math problem is incorrect, but moving **two** sticks will make it correct. Which **two** should be moved?

Start

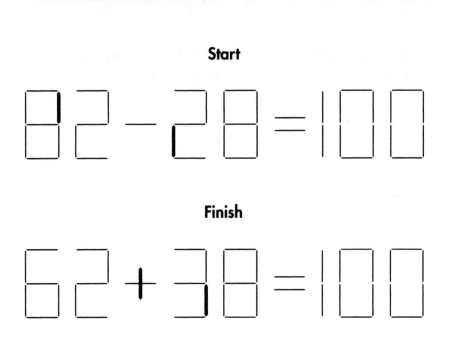

82 − 28 = 100

Finish

62 + 38 = 100

This Roman-numeral math problem is incorrect, but moving **one** stick will make it correct. Which **one** should be moved?

$$XIII = VII - VI$$

Start

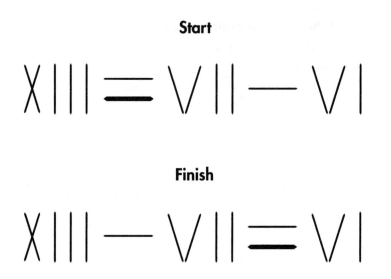

XIII = VII — VI

Finish

XIII — VII = VI

This Roman-numeral math problem is incorrect, but moving **one** stick will make it correct. Which **one** should be moved?

$$X = VII - III$$

Start

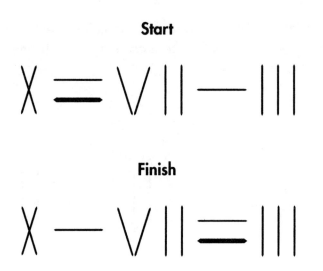

Finish

$$X - VII = III$$

This Roman-numeral math problem is incorrect, but moving **one** stick will make it correct. Which **one** should be moved?

$$XI + V = V$$

Start

$$XI + V = V$$

Finish

$$XI - V = VI$$

Words and Numbers

A long, long time ago in a small village in the north of China, the peasants knew that in the village pond there were two types of creatures—frogs and *chans.* The peasants were able to count a total of **3,600** creatures with a total of **13,000** legs in their pond.

Can you figure out how many frogs and how many *chans* there were in the pond?

(A *chan* is a three-legged froglike mythical creature, which was believed to bring good fortune).

Start

If all the **3,600** creatures in the pond were frogs, there would have been a total of **14,400** legs, which is **1,400** legs more than the peasants counted. Since we know that a *chan* has only three rather than four legs, we can arrive at the correct answer by the following computation.

Finish

First, if there were only frogs, then

3,600 creatures x 4 legs = 14,400 legs

But the leg count is 13,000.

14,400 legs – 13,000 legs = 1,400 legs
in the pond

If, for instance, there were 1,400 *chans*, and the remaining creatures were frogs, then

3,600 creatures – 1,400 *chans* = 2,200 frogs

Therefore:

1,400 *chans* x 3 legs = 4,200 legs
2,200 *chans* x 4 legs = 8,800 legs
13,000 legs

Thus, the pond contained **1,400** *chans* and **2,200** frogs.

A long time ago in China, there was a temple on the side of a big mountain. In the temple there were **100** old monks and young monks. Nobody knew the exact number of those who were young and those who were old. What was known was that altogether the monks ate **100** steamed buns for lunch each day, with each old monk eating **3** steamed buns while every **3** young monks shared **1** steamed bun.

Can you figure out the precise number of old and young monks in the temple?

Start

If there were only old monks in the temple, then they would have needed **300** steamed buns. However, since there were only **100** steamed buns, we can safely assume that there must have been more young monks than old monks because young monks ate less than the old monks. From what the problem tells us, we can also assume that the number of young monks has to be divisible by **3**.

Finish

First, let's try a few numbers for young monks that are divisible by 3.

If, for instance, there were 60 young monks, they would have eaten 20 steamed buns, leaving 40 old monks to eat 120 buns.

But there were only 100 steamed buns to go around.

Let's try again. If there were 66 young monks, the remaining 34 old monks alone would have eaten 102 steamed buns, so this we know would not be correct either. But if we start with 75 young monks, who would eat 25 steamed buns, that leaves 75 steamed buns, which divides by 3 perfectly into 25.

Thus, the temple contained **75** young monks and **25** old monks.

There were two peasant families living in the Ming Dynasty who had one urn between them filled with **10** jin of cooking oil. They also had two ladles, one of which could hold **7** jin of oil, while the other could hold only **3** jin.

Using only these containers, how could these two families equally divide their **10** jin of cooking oil?

(A jin is a Chinese measurement.)

Start

The urn had **10** *jin* of cooking oil.

Ladle #1 holds **7** *jin*.

Ladle #2 holds **3** *jin*.

Finish

Pour 7 jin into ladle #1 from the urn.

Pour 3 jin into ladle #2 from ladle #1.

Empty ladle #2 into the urn.

Pour another 3 jin into ladle #2 from ladle #1.

Empty ladle #2 into the urn again.

Empty ladle #1 (1 jin) into ladle #2.

Pour 7 jin into ladle #1 from the urn.

Fill up the ladle #2 from ladle #1.

Empty ladle #2 into the urn.

Thus, there are **5** *jin* in ladle #1 and **5** *jin* in the urn.

A poor peasant who lived a simple life in the north of China set out to the market one day with a basket of vegetables, a goat, and a wolf to sell. When they came to the Black Dragon River, there was such a narrow bridge that the peasant could cross it with only one of his commodities at a time. The peasant's dilemma was that he dared not leave the vegetable basket alone with the goat, nor the goat alone with the wolf, lest they be eaten before he returned.

How did the peasant take the vegetables, the goat, and the wolf across the bridge without losing anything for the market?

Start

If the goat were left alone with the vegetables, it would eat them. If the wolf were left alone with the goat, it would eat the goat.

Finish

The peasant first crossed the bridge with the goat, and then he went back for the wolf. But once he had crossed with the wolf, he took the goat back with him over the bridge. Leaving the goat behind, he took the vegetable basket. Only after the vegetable basket was safely across with the wolf did the peasant come back one more time and recross with the goat.

Here is a diagram of the peasant's trips across the bridge:

Peasant crosses with goat ⟶

⟵ Peasant crosses back alone

Peasant crosses with wolf ⟶

⟵ Peasant leads goat back

Peasant carries vegetable ⟶
basket across

⟵ Peasant crosses back alone

Peasant leads goat across ⟶

Peasant, goat, wolf, and vegetable basket are all across the bridge and safe.

One day the Monkey King Sun Wukung, his comrade Zhubajie the Pig, and the monk Tangzen were walking through a village on their way to receive the holy Buddist scripture in India when the Monkey King challenged the Pig to a jumping race. Since they were passing through a villlage, the monk proposed that they race from one end of the village threshing ground, which was 50 yards long, to the other and back again. He gave them a choice. One was allowed to take only **2** jumps of **3** yards each every five seconds, while the other was allowed to take **3** jumps of **2** yards each every 5 seconds. The Pig chose the former, and the Monkey King the latter.

Who made the winning choice?

Start

Although the Monkey King and the Pig were technically supposed to move the same distance of **100** yards and could jump the same distance each five seconds, the Pig was forced, by having to jump **3** yards each time, to jump *past* the edge of the **50**-yard threshing ground.

Finish

The Pig had not realized that 50 is not divisible by 3, and thus he would waste part of 2 jumps. The Monkey King had realized that since 50 was divisible by 2, the number of yards he was allowed to go in each jump, he would not waste any part of any jump.

The Monkey King made the winning choice.

One day an Imperial engineer was ordered by the Emperor to measure the length of a road. However, the engineer had only a single piece of rope and he did not know its exact length. What he was able to learn, however, was that if he stretched this rope out on the road **30** times, it was **2** meters too long. But if he stretched the rope out only **29** times, it was **4** meters short of the end of the road.

Can you figure out the length of both the rope and the road?

Start

30 lengths of rope is 2 meters too long.

29 lengths of rope is 4 meters too short.

Finish

If only one more length of rope were added to 29 lengths, it would be 6 meters long.

$$2 \text{ meters} + 4 \text{ meters} = 6 \text{ meters}$$

Therefore, to calculate the length of the road,

$$(6 \text{ meters} \times 30 \text{ lengths}) - 2 \text{meters} = 178 \text{ meters}$$

Thus, the rope is **6** meters long and the road is **178** meters long.

One day while inspecting workers unloading grain from several boats on a rocky river bank, the Bandit King Cao Cao decided to test the intelligence of one of his sons by asking him if he could measure the weight of an elephant that was nearby. Unfortunately, the only scale available was a small one used for weighing sacks of grain.

How did the son satisfy Cao Cao's order, using nothing more than what was around him?

Start

There were several boats on the river.
There were several sacks of grain.
There was also a small scale.

Finish

The Bandit King's son solved the problem by first putting the elephant into a boat and then marking the water line. He then took the elephant out of the boat and loaded the boat with sacks of grain until the boat sank to exactly the same level in the water as when the elephant was on board. Lastly, he directed the workmen to weigh each sack of grain he had put into the boat using the small scale. He then tallied the total weight of all the individual sacks of grain and arrived at the weight of the elephant.

More
Chinese
Brain
Twisters

57 Fast, Fun
Puzzles That Help
Children Develop
Quick Minds

Baifang

Contents

Introduction

There is wisdom in the old Chinese saying "Things learned during childhood remain with one forever." When I was growing up in the north of China during the 1950s and 1960s, my family and friends taught me how to do many of the puzzles included in this book. My parents later recalled others from their childhood in the 1930s and 1940s.

Such puzzles are part of China's folk culture. They have endured for centuries, even through the Communist era of Mao Zedong, when so many other traditional ways of life were lost. They speak of the commitment of Chinese parents to expand their children's intellectual capacities during even their earliest years.

I was very pleased that the first volume of this collection has been so well received and that the publisher was eager for another. I was happy to oblige. I hope you and your children enjoy these puzzles as much as I have.

Baifang

Instructions

The book is divided into two parts: Sticks and Shapes, and Lines, Shapes, and Numbers. Each contains puzzles that help develop agile, creative minds. These mental calisthenics will also help prepare your child for a lifetime of clear, logical thinking. Playing with real sticks allows your child to manipulate the concepts and leads to even greater learning.

Who can solve these puzzles?

Anyone above the age of eight can enjoy the puzzles. When I was a child, my family introduced me to the easiest ones first. As I learned how to solve them, I tried to remember the solutions so that I could solve them faster the next time I saw them.

Although your child may work his or her way through the book alone, it is much more fun to share the experience. You can do these puzzles together at any place, at almost any time—at home, on vacation, on a plane or train, or even while camping. One person can work on them alone, of course, or a group can turn them into a game by competing against each other or against the clock.

What do you need to solve the puzzles?

You'll need a pen or pencil, some paper, and a flat surface. You'll also need about fifty short sticks. Toothpicks or matchsticks are just the right length. You can also use straws cut into equal lengths, about two inches long.

To solve the puzzles, form the patterns with your sticks or draw them on a piece of paper.

Rules for the puzzles:

To **move** sticks means to shift the position of a stick without reducing the original number.

To **remove** a given number of sticks means to take away, thus reducing the number of sticks in the pattern.

To **add** means to increase a given number of sticks.

Let's try one stick puzzle together:

These **three** diamonds can be changed to **four** equilateral (equal-sided) triangles by moving **two** sticks. Which **two** should be moved?

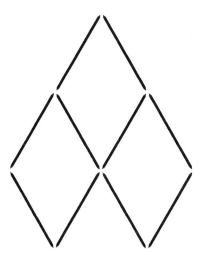

Turn the page to find the solution.

SOLUTION

Start

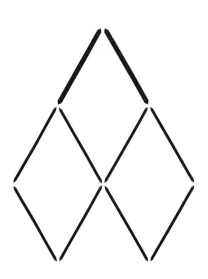

Here the thick lines show the sticks to be moved.

Finish

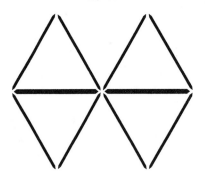

And here the thick lines show the new position of the moved sticks.

Now let's begin!

Sticks and Shapes

By moving **two** sticks, the pattern below can be changed into a dinner fork. Which **two** should be moved?

Start

Finish

Can you form **two** A's using only **four** sticks?

Start

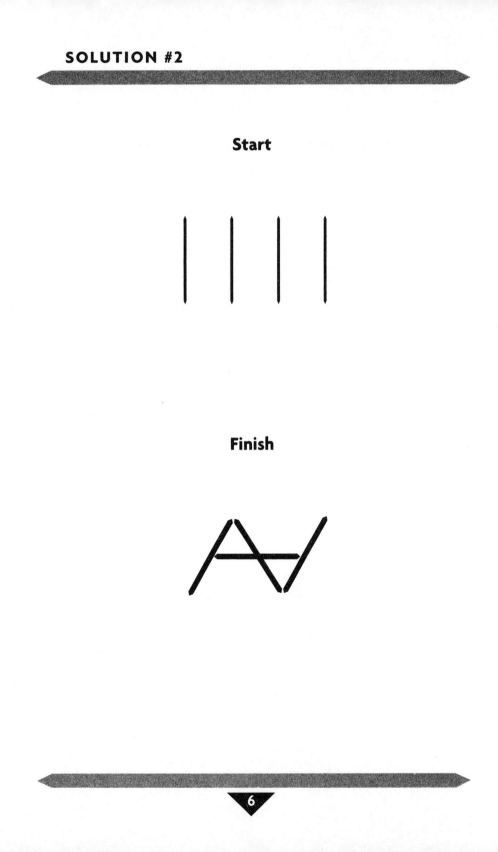

Finish

Can you form **six** triangles and **one** diamond using only these **six** sticks?

Start

Finish

You can make the reflection of the pattern below by moving only **six** sticks. Which **six** need to be moved?

Start

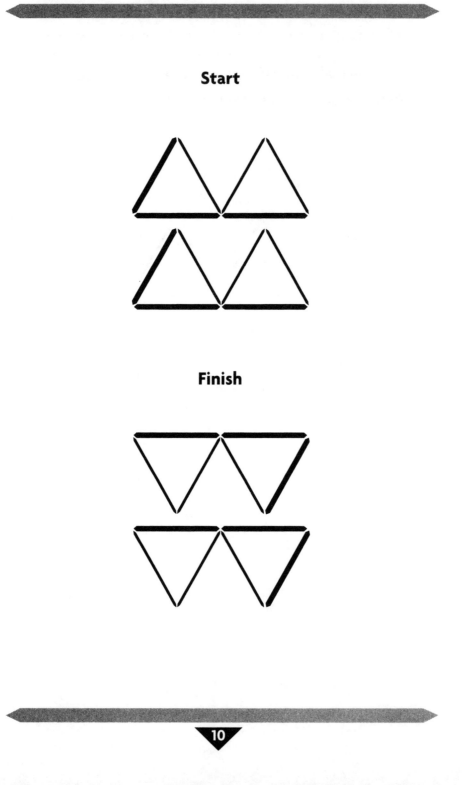

Finish

Please change the pattern on the top to the one on the bottom by moving only **three** sticks. Which **three** ought to be moved?

Start

Finish

How can you form **one** square and **two** diamonds by using **nine** sticks?

Start

Finish

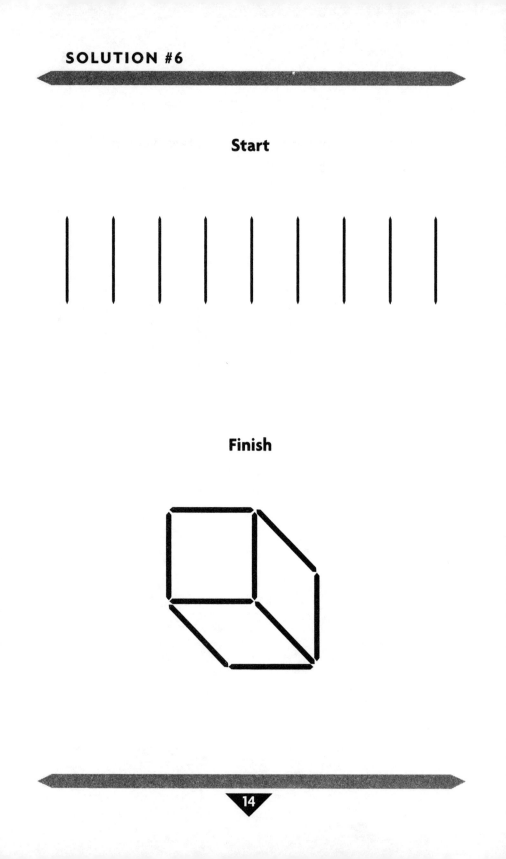

How can you use these **six** sticks to form **eight** triangles?

Start

Finish

How can you form **four** triangles by using only **six** sticks?

| | | | | | |

Start

Finish

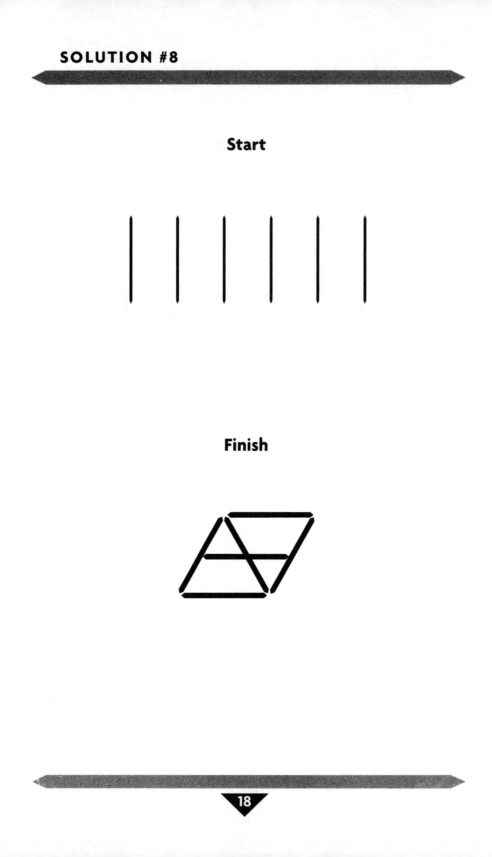

By rearranging **ten** sticks, you can form **five** equal-size triangles and **two** pentagons. How do you do this?

| | | | | | | | | | |

Start

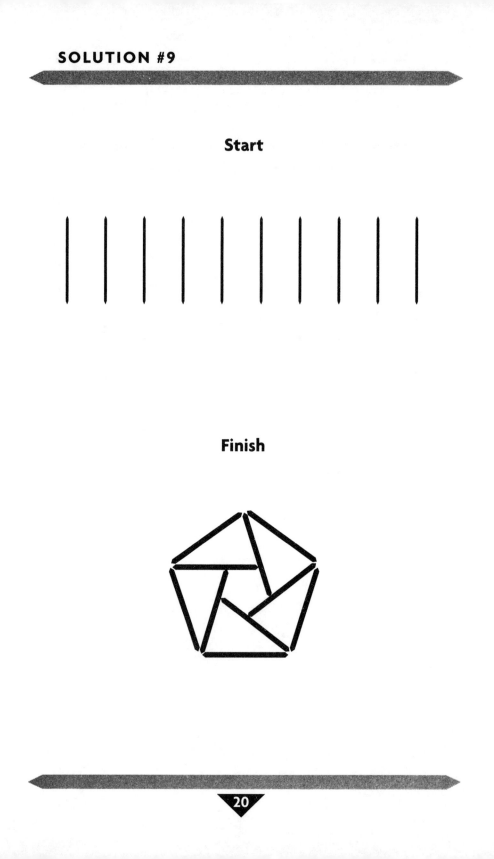

Finish

How can you use **twelve** sticks to form **two** squares and **two** diamonds?

| | | | | | | | | | | | |

Start

Finish

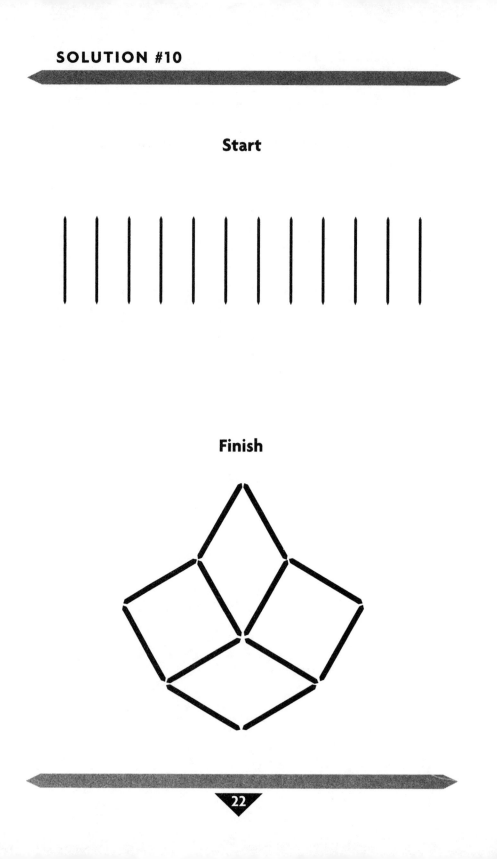

How can you turn the chair away from you by moving only **two** sticks?

Start

Finish

You can turn the chair over onto its back by moving only **three** sticks. Which **three** should be moved?

Start

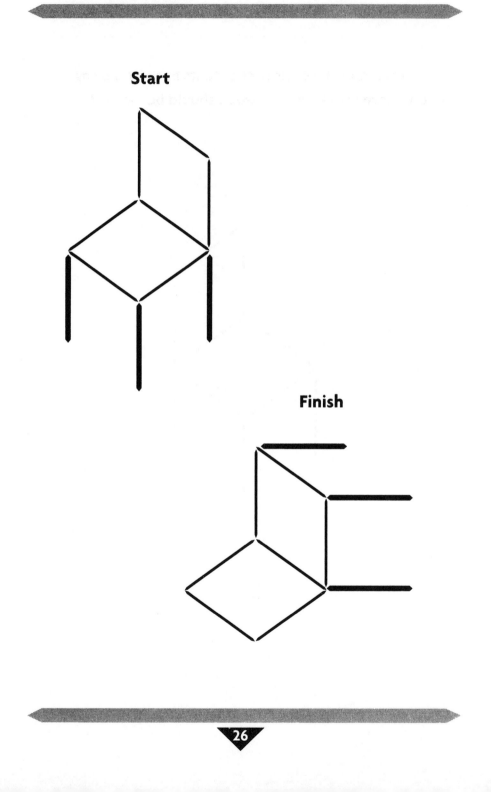

Finish

This dog was run over by a truck. By moving only **two** sticks, you can illustrate this unfortunate fact. Which **two** sticks should be moved?

Start

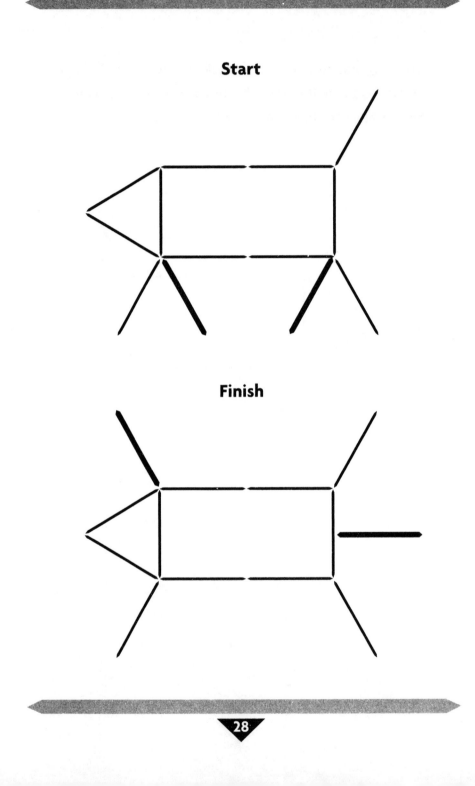

Finish

This big square is formed by **twelve** sticks. By adding **seven** more sticks, you can separate the square into **three** equal parts. Four of the **seven** are already in position. Where should the **three** remaining sticks go?

Start

Finish

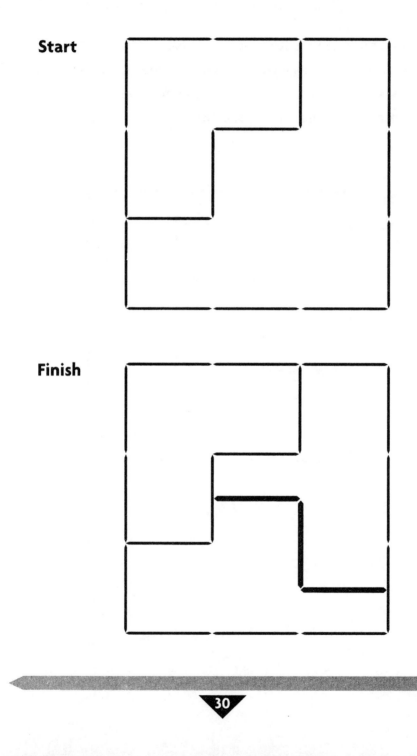

This big shovel can be turned into **two** small shovels by moving **four** sticks. Which **four** need to be moved?

Start

Finish

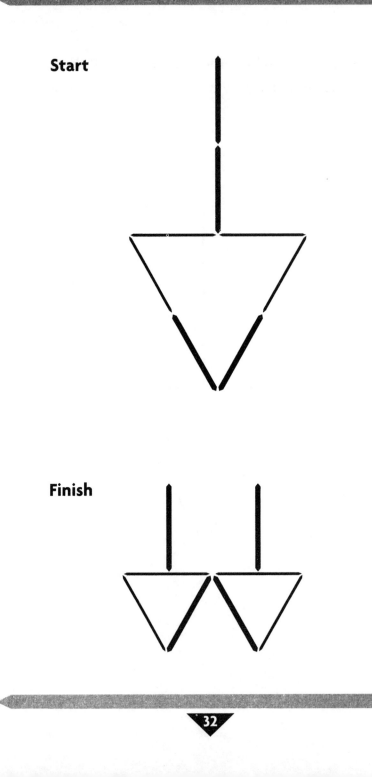

How can you change these **five** equal-size squares into **four** equal-size squares by moving only **four** sticks?

Start

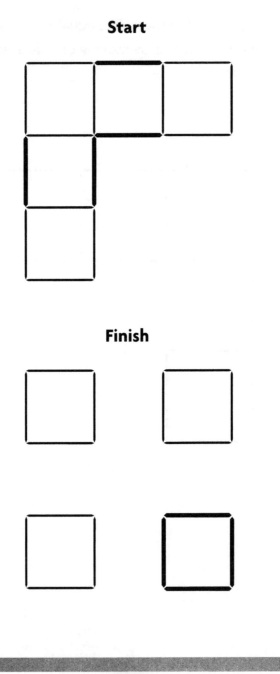

Finish

You can change these **five** equal-size squares into
three squares by moving only **four** sticks. Which **four**
should be moved?

Start

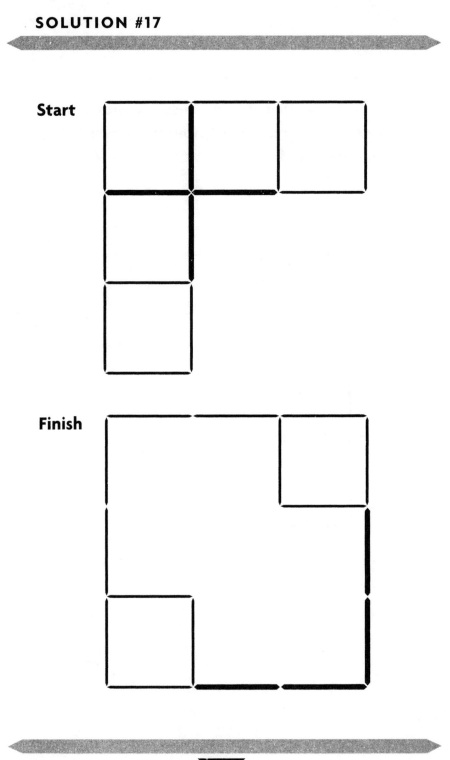

Finish

Forty sticks can be used to form a pattern made up of sixteen equal-size squares. By removing eight sticks, this pattern will have only two squares left. Which eight sticks should be removed?

Start

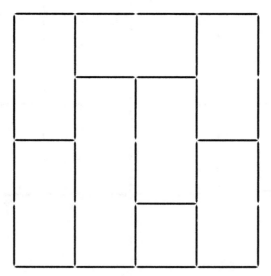

Finish

How can you turn the pattern below upside down by moving only **four** sticks?

Start

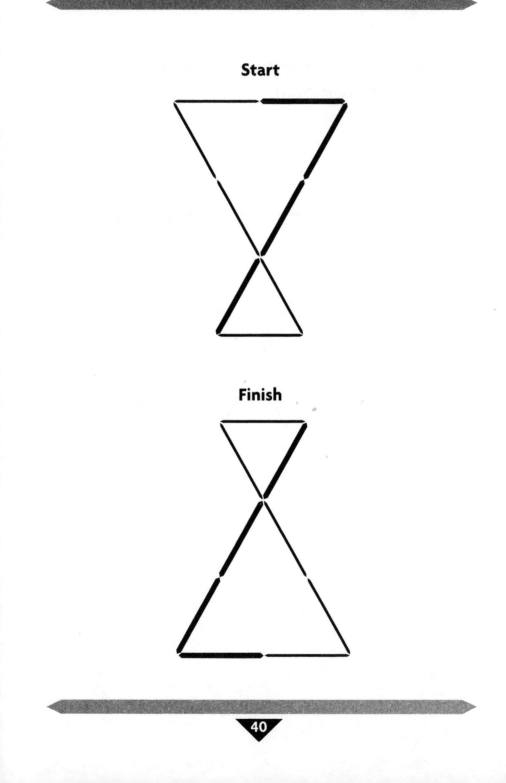

Finish

Here are **two** equal-size diamonds standing side by side. By moving **four** sticks, **one** diamond will disappear and **one** will grow. Which **four** sticks should be moved?

Start

Finish

A pattern with **two** diamonds can be formed by using **seven** sticks. A pattern with **five** diamonds can be formed by using **twelve** sticks. How can you form a pattern with **three** diamonds by using **nine** sticks?

two diamonds

five diamonds

three diamonds (nine sticks)

The pattern below is formed by using **nine** sticks. By removing **two** sticks only **two** equilateral triangles will remain. Which **two** sticks should be removed?

Start

Finish

How can you make this kite fly in the opposite direction by moving only **four** sticks?

Start

Finish

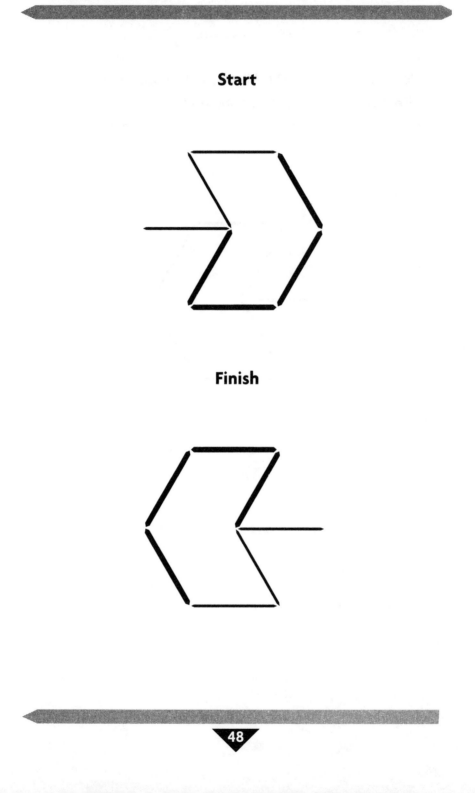

The pattern below is composed of **three** equilateral triangles and **two** squares. How can you rearrange these sticks to form exactly the same number of equilateral triangles and squares in a different pattern?

Start

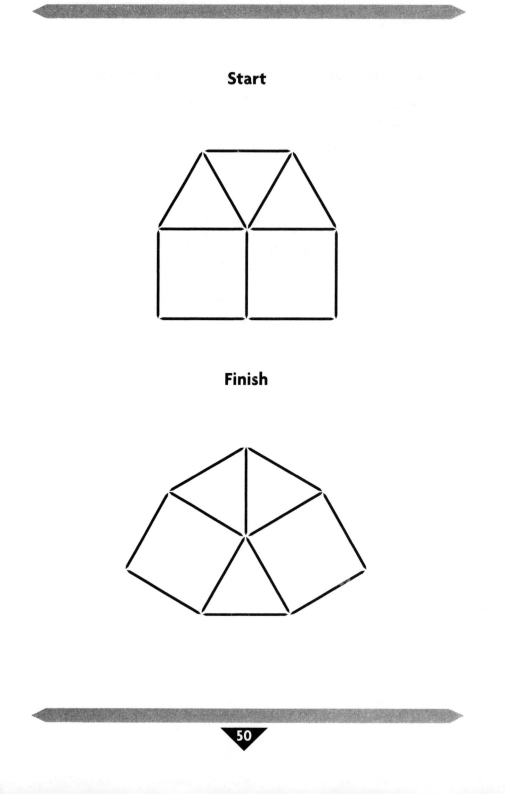

Finish

By moving only **three** sticks, the pattern below will turn upside down. Which **three** sticks should be moved?

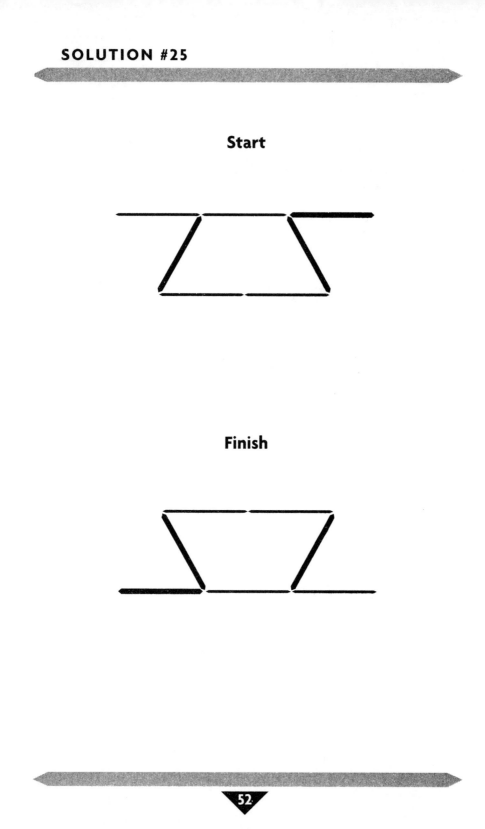

Start

Finish

How can you transform this hexagon into **two** parallelograms by moving **two** sticks and adding **one** more stick?

Start

Finish

added stick

These **five** patterns are formed using same number of sticks. Which pattern has the largest area?

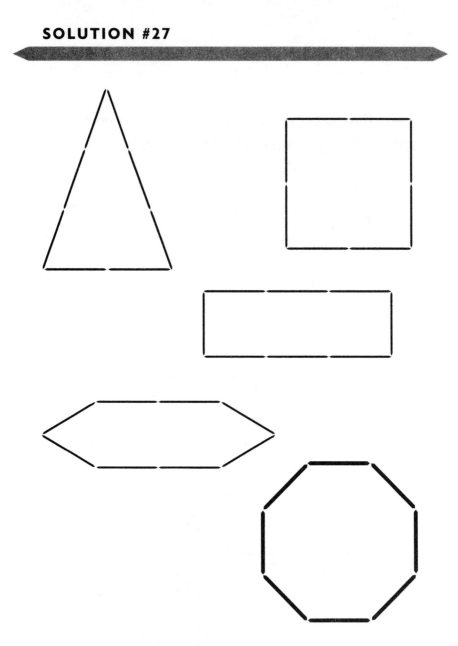

The pattern with a circumference closest to a circle has the largest area. Here the octagon is closest to a circle, so it has the largest area.

There are two ways of adding **six** more sticks to the pattern below so that it will emerge as a new pattern with **five** similarly shaped components. Where should the **six** sticks be placed?

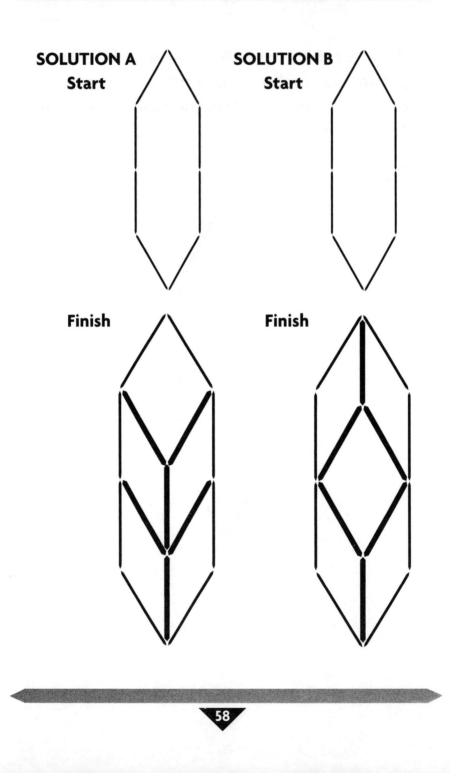

SOLUTION A
Start

SOLUTION B
Start

Finish

Finish

The pattern below has **six** diamonds in it. How can you remove **six** sticks and then resposition **six** other sticks so that the pattern still has **six** diamonds?

Start

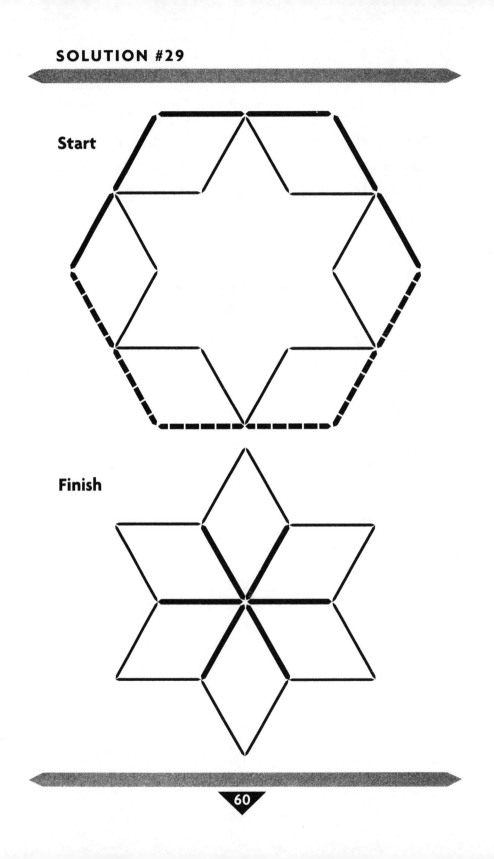

Finish

The pattern below contains **four** equal-size squares.

A. How do you remove **two** sticks so that it will turn into only **two** squares?

B. How do you move **three** sticks so it will turn into **three** squares?

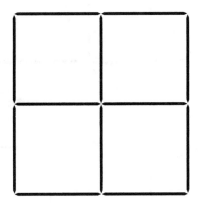

SOLUTION A
Start

SOLUTION B
Start

Finish

Finish

This spiral pattern is made up of **twenty-four** sticks. How do you move **three** sticks to turn the spiral into **three** squares?

Start

Finish

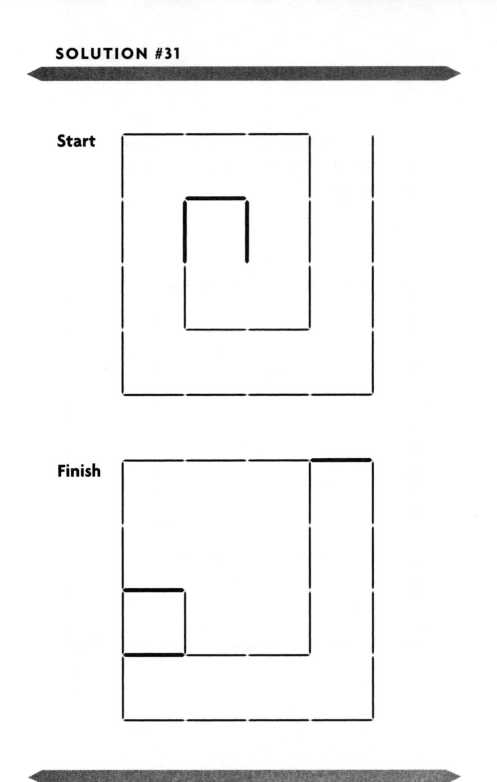

The pattern below contains **seven** equal-size squares. If you move **three** sticks it turns into only **five** equal-size squares. Which **three** sticks should be moved?

Start

Finish

Lines, Shapes, and Numbers

How can you connect all the dots below and make the bottom shape with **one** continuous stroke? You're not allowed to trace over any lines!

Start

Finish

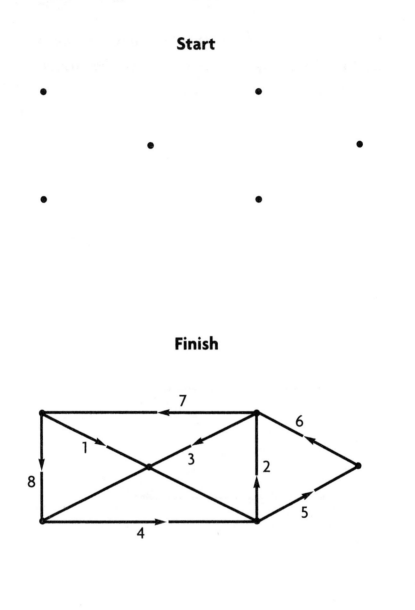

How can you connect all the dots below and make the bottom shape with **one** continuous stroke? You're not allowed to trace over any lines!

Start

Finish

The equation below is incorrect, but it can be corrected by moving only **three** sticks on the left side of the equation. Which **three** sticks should you move?

$$1351 - 900 = 1991$$

Start

Finish

The equation below is incorrect, but it can be corrected by moving only **one** stick. Which stick should be moved?

Start

Finish

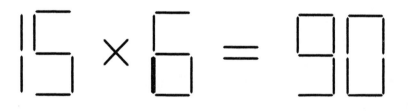

Below are **two** shapes. **One** has already been divided into **two** halves. How can you divide the other into **two** pieces so that when the **four** pieces are put together you will form a square?

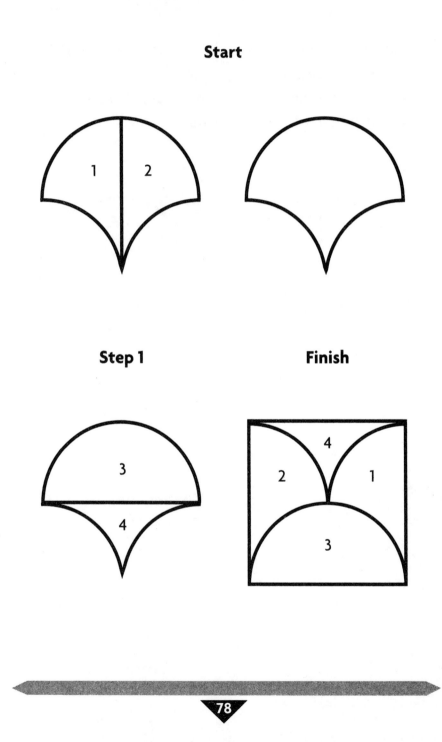

Start

Step 1

Finish

The pattern below is made up of **three** equal-size squares. There is a dot in the center of **one** square. Please draw a line over the dot so that the area on either side of the line will be equal.

Start

Finish

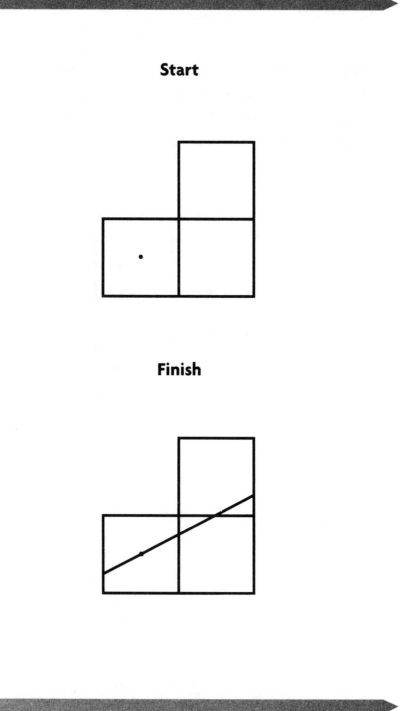

Please add the math symbols: $+$, $-$, $\times$, ( ), and $=$ among the numbers **1** through **9** so that when you calculate the equation it will equal **100**.

$$1 \quad 2 \quad 3 \quad 4 \quad 5 \quad 6 \quad 7 \quad 8 \quad 9 = 100$$

Start

$$1 \quad 2 \quad 3 \quad 4 \quad 5 \quad 6 \quad 7 \quad 8 \quad 9 = 100$$

Finish

$$(1 + 2 + 3 + 4 + 5) \times 6 - 7 + 8 + 9 = 100$$

Please use **eight 8s** to form **five** numbers, then add the **five** numbers together. The sum of the **five** numbers should be **1,000.**

8   8   8   8   8   8   8   8

Start

8   8   8   8   8   8   8   8

Finish

$$888 + 88 + 8 + 8 + 8 = 1,000$$

When you add **one** line to **one** triangle, it turns into **three** triangles. When you add **two** lines, **six** triangles emerge. How many triangles will you have when you add **three** lines to the triangle?

Start

Finish

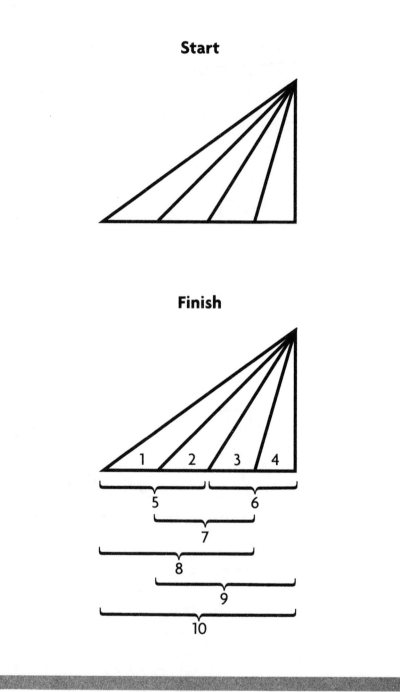

How many triangles are there in the pattern below?

Start

Finish There is a total of 27 triangles.

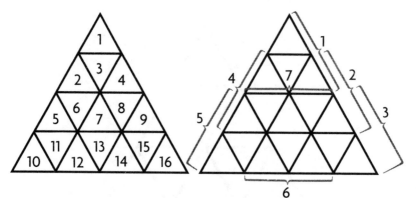

16 small ones

7, each made of 4 small ones

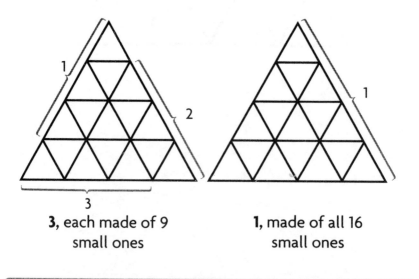

3, each made of 9
small ones

1, made of all 16
small ones

The number formed by these **three** blocks is **136.** This number cannot be divided by **7.** Please rearrange these **three** blocks so that the new number can be divided by **7.**

Start

Finish

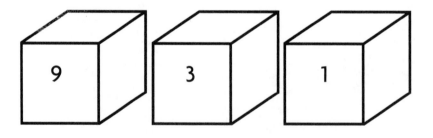

Each of the **six** sides of the following blocks is painted with a color. With these **three** sides shown, can you figure out the color of the opposite sides that are not shown?

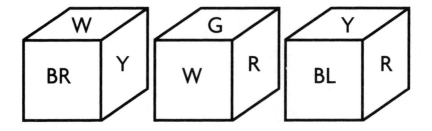

White is opposite blue;
red is opposite brown;
yellow is opposite green.

Find the pattern to the numbers in the circle below,
then fill in the correct number in the empty space.

Start

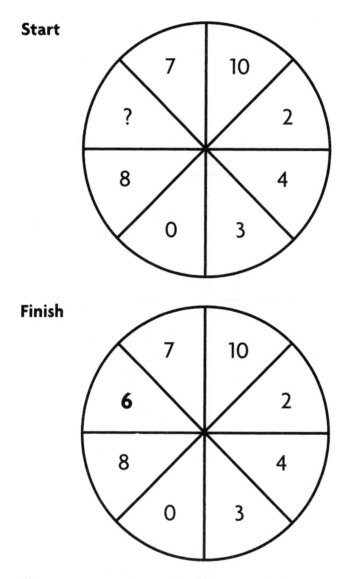

Finish

The correct number is **6.** (The sum of the numbers on opposite sides of the pie is **10.**)

Find the pattern to the numbers in the rectangle below, then fill in the correct number in the empty space.

9	8	5
81	64	25
63	48	?

Column 1   **Column 2**   **Column 3**

Start

Column 1	Column 2	Column 3
9	8	5
81	64	25
63	48	?

Finish

Column 1	Column 2	Column 3
9	8	5
81	64	25
63	48	**15**

The correct number is **15**. (The second number of each column minus double the first number equals the third number.)

Please fill in the numbers **1, 2, 3,** and **4** in the blank spaces below so that this math problem will make sense.

Start

Finish

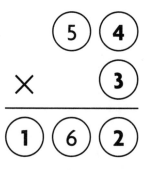

The **two** columns below are made up of circles with numbers in them. By switching **two** circles and adding a little cleverness, the sum of the **two** columns will become equal. How do you do this?

Start

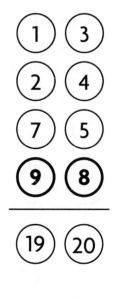

Finish

Switch circles 8 and 9, and then flip the 9 to 6.

Take **ten** sticks and put them side by side. Pick up **one** stick and jump over **two** others to form a pair with a third stick. Make **five** separate jumps over two sticks to end up with five paired sticks. A pair of sticks counts as two as you jump over them. Hint: The first jump involves stick #4.

SOLUTION #49

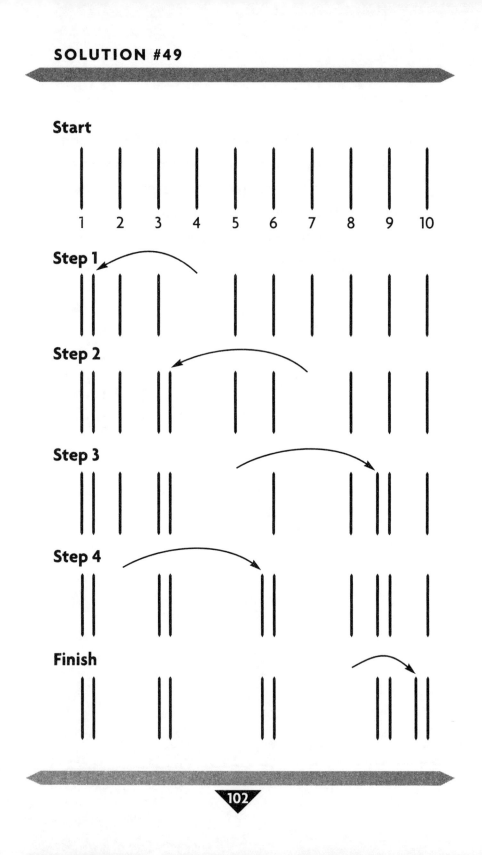

Start

1 2 3 4 5 6 7 8 9 10

Step 1

Step 2

Step 3

Step 4

Finish

The pattern below consists of **one** big triangle and **three** small triangles. How do you fill in numbers **1** through **9** around the big triangle so that the sum of the numbers in the corners of each triangle equals **15**?

Start

Finish

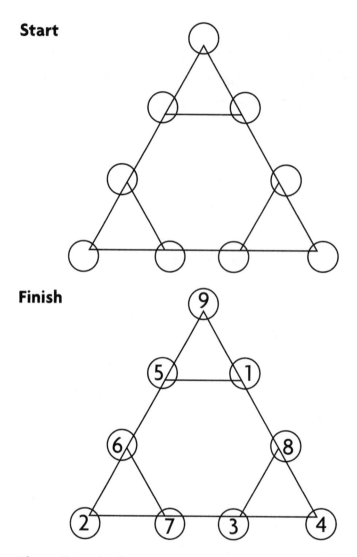

There is more than one arrangement of numbers that solves the puzzle, although the three corners of the big triangle must be 9, 2, and 4.

How can you fill in the **nine** small squares with numbers **1** through **9** so that the sum of all **three** numbers—horizontally, vertically, and diagonally—is the same?

Start

Finish

4	9	2
3	5	7
8	1	6

There is more than one arrangement of numbers that solves this problem.

Discover the pattern of how the numbers are
increasing, then fill in the blank space.

(3) (5) (9) $(?)$ (23) (33) (45)

Start

③ ⑤ ⑨ ? ㉓ ㉝ ㊺

Finish

③ ⑤ ⑨ **15** ㉓ ㉝ ㊺

$3 + 1\,(2) = 5$; $5 + 2\,(2) = 9$; $9 + 3\,(2) = 15$; $15 + 4\,(2) = 23$; and so on.

Connect these **five** chains together to form a big chain ring. Only **four** rings can be opened. How can you do this?

Start

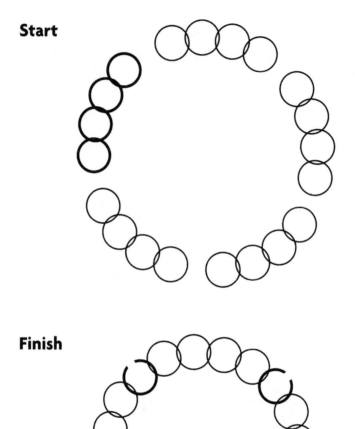

Finish

Open one chain of rings to connect the other **four** chains.

Remove a small triangle from both the white and the black portions of the pattern below. Then place the white triangle on the black side, and the black triangle on the white side, so that the pattern will turn into **two** fishes. Where do you cut then place the triangles?

Start

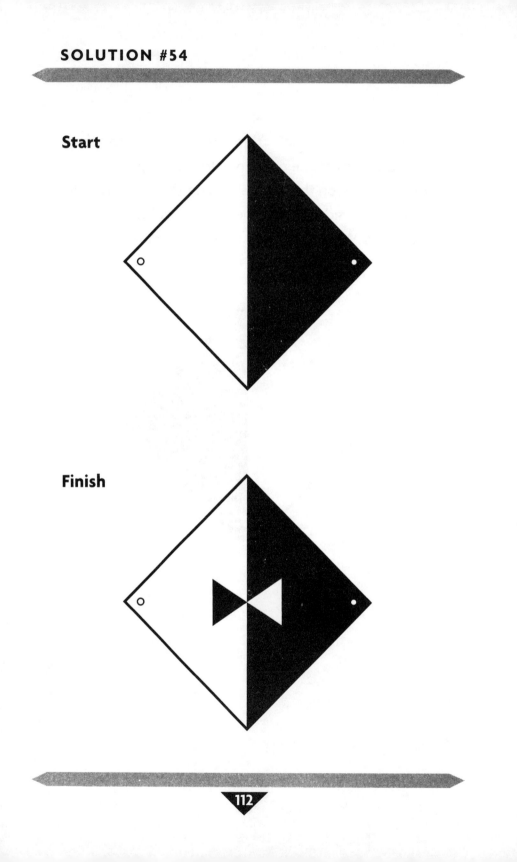

Finish

How do you separate the big H below into **five** pieces with two lines and then use those pieces to form a square?

Start

Step 1   **Finish**

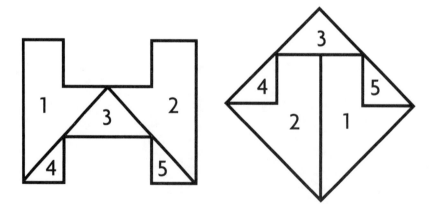

You can separate the pattern below into **three** pieces and then use those pieces to form a **five**-pointed star. How can you do this?

Start

Step 1

Finish

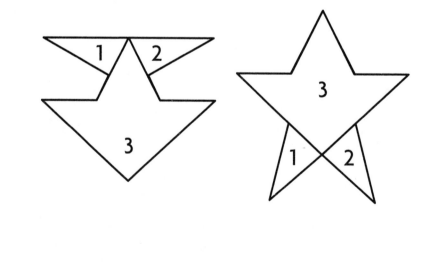

How do you separate the **two** squares into **four** pieces and then use those pieces to form **one** square?

Start

Step 1

Finish

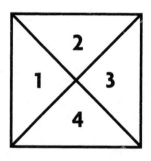